IT TAKES LONGER THAN a Day

A Guide to Effectively Building Relationships with Students

Demetric Blankinship

ISBN: 978-1-960853-87-5

Liberation's Publishing House
Columbus, Mississippi

This book is dedicated to those educators who have the desire to save each child that enters his or her classroom from the uncommon or unfamiliar places in life. Take a deep breath, remain focused, hold tight to your passion, and remember- it CAN happen but just not in one day.

BLOOM WITH GRACE

Table of Contents

01 PROLOGUE

Because I know educators are so bogged down with work outside the classroom and time is so limited, I would like to offer you, in just a few pages, a guide on how to build effective and meaningful relationships with your students.

We have all, at some point, heard the phrase, "Insanity is doing the same thing over and over and expecting a different result." Oftentimes, educators find themselves in this exact dilemma. Each day, we wake up with the mindset to make it the best day ever inside the classroom. We tend to plan our day and week through lesson plans and mentally rehearse the activities ahead. The plan seems perfect, and in our minds, the day ends full of joy and achievement.

However, the plans fail. The day ends in a whirlwind. We consider quitting the job and not returning the next day. The process of browsing Indeed's job site and applying for another position begins—all while we are still confined within the classroom. Failure is all we see. In that moment, we are seeking what feels like the easiest way out.

Surprisingly, no one can talk us out of this mindset when we're in it. Yet deep inside, we know there is a purpose and a plan behind why we initially took on the role of an educator. It is at that moment that we begin rehearsing the activities for the next day—without acknowledging that we're planning to do the exact same thing that left us feeling like complete failures.

So, the questions educators often plunder are as follows:

1
How can I change my routine so that I can be effective?

2
What am I doing wrong that is causing my day and myself to feel like a total reject?

3
Why am I so out of touch with my students?

4
Lord, is this the plan You have for me?

The list could go on, but these are the questions that surface so easily and rapidly.

The goal of this book is to serve as a guide for those who have the desire to excel in their current capacity as educators. When the term excel is mentioned, it does not merely refer to excelling as a teacher of a subject; it also emphasizes excelling in building lasting, ethical bonds and relationships with students—bonds that will drive academic, social, mental, and moral success.

As you read these pages, take note of the ideas presented. Function as a student by highlighting the areas you find most important and making note of the areas in which you may need improvement.

The question I want you to ask yourself is:

"How can I use the time and resources I have to become a champion in the life of my students?"

Task 1

How can I use the time and resources I have available to become a champion in the life of my students?

_____

_____

_____

_____

_____

_____

_____

_____

_____

_____

_____

_____

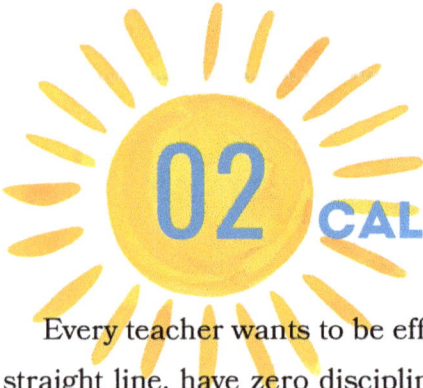

02 CALLING OR CAREER

Every teacher wants to be effective, make his or her students walk the straight line, have zero discipline referrals, obtain the highest academic scores, and become Teacher of the Year at least once. More often, however, every educator wants to be a hero. Is this really feasible in today's education system? The answer is yes. Educators are everyday heroes, even when they have experienced what may seem to be the most horrific and stressful day, week, month, or year—for some. But the reality of the issue is that educators do not always see themselves as heroes because they want to walk into the classroom and save every little Mark and Sue from every academic issue and any issue that may be surfacing from the home front. The hard part of the scenario is, educators can save students from many of the perils of life, but it just cannot be done in one academic workday.

~Callings draw the resources and time needed to fulfill the mission~

When there is a call over your life, and it surfaces over into your chosen career, you will be equipped with all you need to overcome even the harshest situations. However, when it is just a career and you are in the process of doing the same thing repeatedly, you will not be able to effectively make impactful decisions. You will instead be found doing only the bare minimum, which will not be effective for your students, yourself, or your co-workers.

A calling is when love intercedes and allows you to go beyond your call of duty in every encounter with your student. A calling will keep you wide awake many nights with your student Sue on your mind, contemplating how you are going to be able to reach her and peel through the anger she has built up inside—even though she is a true academic genius. A calling will cause you to think of creative ways to reach student Mark, even though the entire district has deemed Mark a complete failure because he came from a family of failures. It is in these moments you realize it is no longer just a career but something larger, and often, the problem or crisis at hand is much larger than you. However, this is where you must be willing to make things personal—yet professional, but not personal to a point where you will find yourself on probation or sitting in an administrative hearing.

To reach students, educators must be effective and rapid decision-makers. One must remember the decision you make now will be one that will have lasting impacts on the livelihood of yourself and all the others involved.

Teaching is a matter of the heart, and effort put into teaching must come from the heart and be centered around love and passion. A successful and impactful teacher loves what he or she sets out to do each day. If he or she does not love what they are doing, each day, at the sound of the alarm, excuses will surface as to why the day will be dreaded even before it starts.

Not only will we dread the surface, but excuses will become increasingly present. Before entering the classroom, the educator's mind is made up that the day before them will be awful. Students and colleagues have already been identified as direct targets. Anxiety will cause one to be all over the place, and any little trigger will lead to chaos for all involved.

Is this truly the image you want to carry? Because, rather apparent or not, others see your dismal and dreadful situation. Not to mention, your negative energy is contagious.

ATTRACT POSITIVITY

Task 2

Of all the career paths you could have chosen, why did you decide becoming a teacher was more favorable for you?

_____

_____

_____

_____

_____

_____

_____

_____

_____

_____

_____

_____

03 THE WHY BEHIND YOUR CAREER CHOICE

The biblical scripture, "Many are called but a very few are chosen," can also be asserted into context with the careers and paths we take on in life. Due to having summers off, Spring Break, and other holidays, many people easily dive into the educational career sector. They consider the short workday, being home with their children, and, in some cases, the ability to be on campus with their children. However, very few take into consideration the workloads associated with education, the unwarranted stress that often arises, the duty of being responsible for an entire classroom or grade level of students, and the dedication that goes into building relationships with students.

Teaching is a work of the heart and not something that can be taught or learned to successfully execute through the reading of textbooks or sitting in long lectures. Recent studies have shown that teaching is more of a calling than an everyday clock-in and clock-out career. The forefront and foundation of teaching is love. To be successful as an educator, one must bear the fruits of the Spirit, which are love, joy, peace, patience, kindness, faithfulness, gentleness, and self-control.

~few take into consideration the workloads associated with education~

8

When growing up, I never once told a single person I wanted to "be a teacher when I grow up." Nor did teaching ever cross my mind, but here I am, eleven years later, "killing it," as the younger generation says. My passion was law and government, which later led to law enforcement and corrections. However, no matter how many degrees I obtained trying to move up the ladder in Criminal Justice Administration, I was never happy nor content. Something was missing, and, at the time, I did not know what it was. I do know during any free time, I always found myself in the presence of both children and adults, offering academic services. I could never turn anyone away. My response was always, "Yes," or "As soon as I am available, I will make contact to schedule a time to help you." In addition, each time, I could feel a strong passion for rendering the services I was providing.

In what seemed like a matter of moments, life-changing events occurred. I had to re-evaluate choices made in life, decisions had to be made, and I had to unexpectedly step into the unknown. In what seemed like a matter of seconds, I found myself in the position of a teacher's assistant, in a school district that was poverty-stricken, and I knew absolutely no one. There was no prior knowledge or any experience, other than the "homegrown" services I had provided to individuals within my community and surrounding communities. "Life was lifing," but God was Godding and encamping angels and mentors all around me. I will never forget two educators by the name of Mrs. Evans and Mrs. Thigpen. I watched daily how they would pour into their students. They would provide academic, as well as spiritual and emotional, support. I would oftentimes reflect upon the educators who had touched me academically and emotionally as a youth. These educators have made all the difference in my life. As I was beginning my career in education, I knew that I, too, wanted to be someone's champion. That opportunity soon came.

A few years later, at the change of school districts, I can remember sitting in an assembly on the first day of school. As I was sitting in my seat, I was still thinking about all the things that I wished I were home still enjoying—you know, the fun things that came with summer break. That year, luckily, I was privileged to be employed with a school district that did not place religion on the back burner. The principal of one of the schools gave an opening prayer and scripture. He then went on to give words of encouragement to all those in attendance. Of all he said on this morning, there was one statement he made that resonated deep within and has remained embodied in my daily thoughts, actions, and deeds. His words were, **"You will maintain where you have been ordained."**

Ordination is special; ordination is spiritual; ordination is personal; and ordination is a task that comes with purposeful love in words and actions. It was that year I answered my ordination as an educator, a difference maker, and a mentor to the many students I would encounter. It was at this moment that I started to create relationships in the classroom, in the community, and with families. I was no longer bound to the stress of test scores and feeling doomed when I was assigned the lower academic achievers. At this moment, I knew there was more to this career than teaching required standards and teaching subjects. I began bonding with my students, creating a classroom climate and culture that were conducive to learning.

Faith and Hope

Then after, my students began to **SOAR** academically and GROW into a wealth of prosperity. Parents and guardians, along with the administrators and coworkers, began to buy into my delivery methods. In the community, I was not known just as the teacher of Reading, but I was the teacher that would show up and the teacher who would humble herself and never consider herself beyond the lives and lifestyles of the community I served. Parents bought into my demeanor and accepted my investment in their child(ren), and they simultaneously got on board. Academics began to SOAR within the classroom, and lasting relationships were established.

As you venture into the next pages, you will find a very informal, yet informative, blueprint on how you, too, can become a champion by making simple adjustments in your classroom. Remember, champions win championships through practice, discipline, and **BELIEVING** in the possibilities of what others see as the impossible.

.

BELIEVE IN YOURSELF

AN EDUCATOR'S
Toolkit
TO SUCCESS

Get to Know
1 Your Students

In a neighboring school district, educators were given the luxury of taking a bus throughout the communities the school district served. In this way, educators were able to see where the students lived, the community or environment they came from, the type of life they had at home, and the personalities of the family. This was a requirement for the district, but if you are like me, you may be employed in a district where this is not an option, and visiting the home of a student may be unethical. Now you ponder the likelihood of getting to know your students. Does it really require visiting their homes and neighborhoods? Definitely not, but it does have its plus side.

Getting to know your students can be as simple as journal entries and free-fall discussions in the classroom. On the first day of school, I do not ask my students to write about what he or she did for the summer because the summer for Mark may have been filled with Mom or Dad—or even both—being incarcerated. Mark may have lost a family member, or Mark may have received only one meal a day for the entire summer and slept most nights on the couch in the bearing heat.

Whereas Sue may have had the opportunity to visit Disney with friends. Her family may have purchased a new home. Sue may have even visited the public library every day with friends and gotten a jumpstart on the academic year.

Prior to really learning the do's and do nots of creating a positive classroom environment, I was that teacher who thought life was peaches and cream for every student. Well, it was not. So, instead of asking students to write on the first day to discuss their summer, I began each class by telling the students how excited I was to start a new academic year. I explained the everyday rules and procedures but informed the students that my goal was to create a safe space for everyone who entered. I elaborated on standards and goals we would set regarding academics but advised that academic goals could only be achieved if we created a safe space—yet a fun space. Students will be interested in the fun part, and all else will follow.

Just before class ends, I would pass around index cards and tell students if they wanted me to know anything interesting about them, they could share it on the card. With this method, students did not feel pressured. At this moment, they are still focused on the word fun. Before you start to wonder, this method was used at the elementary, middle, and high school levels. The word fun goes a long way in education if it is genuine fun. Because they were still focused on the word "fun," they did not mind taking part in this activity.

Now, it is important to remember that life for even children is difficult, and they encounter things that seem unimaginable. Therefore, it is important to remember your scope regarding privacy/confidentiality and your Educator Code of Ethics. It is safe to say that within my 11 years of teaching, I have not experienced any first-day notes that would warrant me contacting the school counselor, administration, Department of Human Services, or local law enforcement.

On the notes, you will find out how many siblings the students have, if they are from a single-parent home, if they live with grandparents, if they have certain medical diagnoses, their favorite sport, their favorite sports team, their future plans—and the list could go on.

Now that you have sold yourself to them, explained how excited you were about the new year, and showed an interest in things in their lives, you have made the first step toward building trust.

It seems too simple, right? Of course it does, and that is the problem with many unsuccessful educators. Sometimes we think too big when the smallest gestures are what matter most.

Not only did you win the student by showing interest, but the fact that you are going to take time to read through these notes shows that you care a lot already and are willing to sacrifice time that could be used elsewhere to read their thoughts, plans, and ideas. Therefore, it is equally important for you to read these ideas in the presence of the students—but not aloud, for privacy concerns. Again, you are showing a fond interest.

Do you realize how many of the students you connect with each day feel unnoticed? Many are silently crying out to be heard through subtle seclusion and intentional isolation because, for so long, no one—not even a parent—has taken notice of them and their needs. The needs can range from physical, social, emotional, and mental oppression.
Here it is—in just a few minutes, you have made some child, or shall I say SCHOLAR, feel alive, included, accepted, and, more importantly, loved.

After the note-writing exercise, you can now incorporate things in your life that connect to the things you have just read on the notes. With this exercise, you are strengthening the already developing relationship. Your scholars will now open up more frequently because they feel you are relatable, yet they recognize you are their classroom superior. They are now making advances toward respect for you that will drive success in every area of your daily classroom operations.

Now that the foundation is poured into the building of this relationship, let us call in other contractors to offer advice and support. Remember, just like a house that cannot be built successfully in one day, neither can we successfully build the perfect academic setting in one day. It takes time, effort, and constant encouragement and reinforcement because every child and every situation are different.

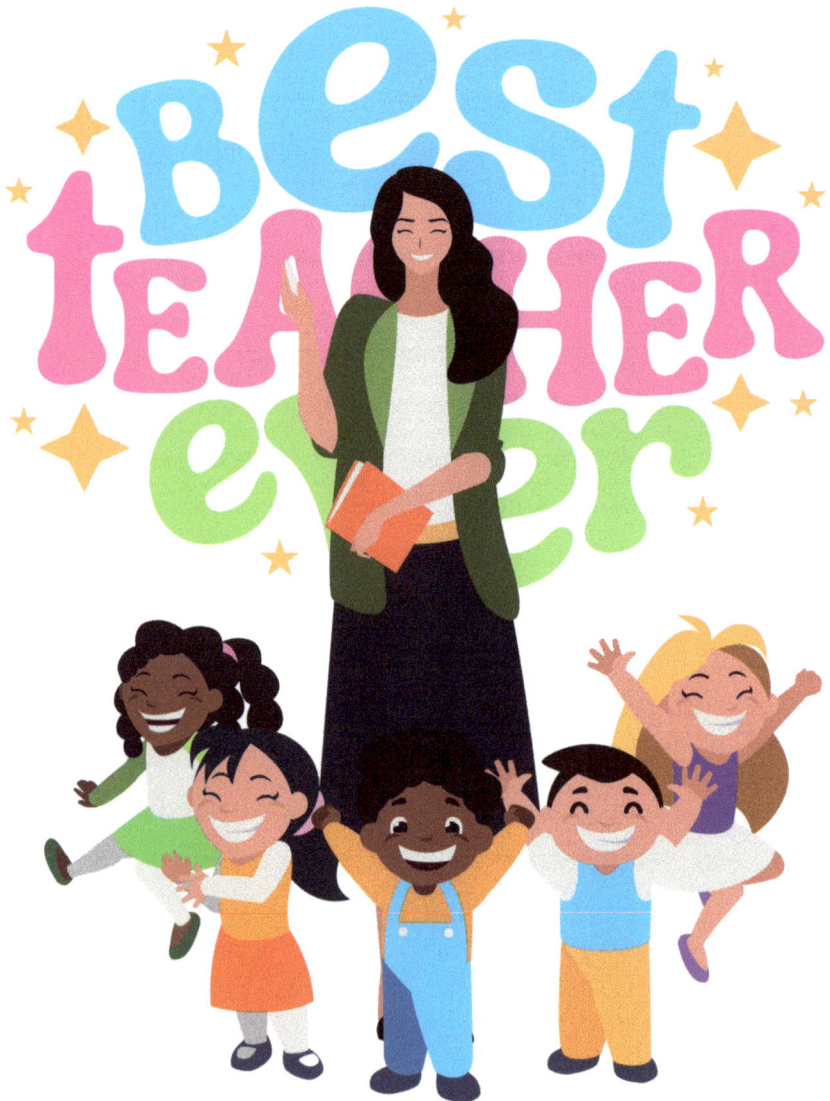

Creating a Family 2 Oriented Classroom

In every classroom I have ever taught in Ole Miss has been my classroom's theme. There is one sign that I will hang first, and it remains for the entire academic year. The sign reads, "Ole Miss Fans Live Here."However, I blot out "Fans" and replace it with "Family." I explain to my students I am a die-hard Ole Miss fan and am optimistic of them too becoming die hard Ole Miss fans.

My next line includes me explaining to them how we will function as a family. We will not hurt one another through actions, thoughts, or deeds-but will make every effort to support one another, as a real family would. We discuss the characteristics of a family and lay out important family values such as honesty, sharing, and love. Again, we are building on this relationship. Students are usually left in shock and awe because for many this is the first time they have inherited these type conversations, especially at the beginning of an academic year or at the first acquaintance of a teacher. Usually, teachers come in off the press with a macho man attitude, trying to act ten feet tall and bullet proof, or just straight out firm and by the book. This all seems different and awkward to the student, but in all reality, it is a good different-awkward situation.

You are now pondering how this family-oriented classroom operates. It is simple, but all parties must buy in. We all have individuals we can pick as leaders from the start. These individuals will serve as our caretakers. They will ensure certain tasks in the classroom are taken care of. They will ensure the computers are passed out daily and placed back in their designated areas after use. You will have someone who is responsible for the pencils being sharpened and placed in the correct location. Someone will be responsible for other tasks such as attendance, restroom routines, keeping time, passing out any worksheets or communications, and the list could go on. With these jobs or assignments, we act like a family in issuing chores. Students once again feel valued, included, and loved. Parents oftentimes think their child or children are lazy, when the truth is they are usually not given the opportunity to prove their positive character traits and feel a part of the family's daily operative routines. Most importantly, we will celebrate each other.

The relationship is getting stronger and stronger, and the scholar now has a desire to be at school each day, because they cannot let the family down by not being present to fulfill his or her responsibilities. If the child is present, learning is taking place. If learning is taking place, the child is sure to be growing academically and responsibly. Look at the gains that are taking place off an initial get to know your student and create a family-oriented environment.

Creating a Classroom Climate
3 and Culture Conducive to Learning

People, adults, and children will always remember how another individual made them feel. You can say things to people, and they will forget or at least forget the exact wording. However, the feeling you impose upon a person will last a lifetime, especially if it is a special type of emotion.

When students enter your classroom, they should feel warmth. This is not warmth regarding heat or temperature. But they should feel the love. They should feel welcome. Your classroom should serve as a safe place. You all became acquainted within the first few moments of class, then you ensured they knew they were a part of a family, now it is time that this family member knows this classroom is home-only in an academic setting. There is no place we should go that takes the place of us feeling like we are at home, right? Remember, not all students come from this luxurious loving home, so school may be the only place they will find the missing pieces to the puzzle of life.

Should the classroom be a place of hostility?

No.

Will there be days when teachers and students feel agitated from life and the happenings of life itself?

Yes.

How can you overcome the two and keep the climate warm and welcoming?

We are not perfect, and the students know this. Our students are not perfect, and we know this. Therefore, GRACE must be rendered inside academic setting. We must be willing to offer each other a little grace, controlling our temper and words. Our scholars will see this, and they will, with more eagerness, want to perform for you now more so than ever. They will put their GRACE inside their academic studies. Let us remember, these tactics are not just for the high achieving students, because in most cases they come from a supportive background and life for them may have some bumps and bruises, but life is not a perfect crystal stair. So, these are methods that will allow us to reach our lower academic achievers.

Will they become "A" students over night or over an academic term?

No. However, they will show substantial growth. Growth is so much more important than remaining complacent in an area.

Now let us talk about...
CULTURE

How does culture make an impact in the academic setting?

Culture helps promote diversity. I am sure you are wondering how this author can talk about culture, when she said in previous pages she used Ole Miss as her Classroom theme. It is simple, I never once used the highly publicized history of Ole Miss in any way to draw or dis-draw my students. What I did was, I used the fact of Ole Miss being my favorite school to draw my students and engage them in a like for learning and a desire to know more about colleges and universities. Every aspect of your classroom should serve as a purpose. By the end of the academic year, students will have been introduced to multiple colleges and universities because I will promote culture, while at the same time systematically helping them develop an interest in continuing their education.

Culture's primary focus in the academic setting is to promote diversity. Promoting diversity, in turn, promotes acceptance. No matter what your background, my primary focus is to educate, inspire, and mentor. This is impossible if an educator is bias in any way or allows their scholars to be bias in any way. Therefore, we must promote culture and make our students, who come from various cultures, lifestyles, and traditions, feel important and know that no matter the background, it has a place in "our" family/classroom. This too is an opportunity to influence learning. We teach various lessons throughout the year, and the opportunity will present itself where we will be able to incorporate the culture of our students. If we create a classroom of culture initially, students will have interest and be less anxious to open to innovative ideas of others' beliefs and backgrounds.

For example:

Black History Month has been nationally recognized for many years. Each year schools put on programs, and Black History in taught through the course of class assignments and lessons. Just imagine the pride a Hispanic student may feel when we incorporate their culture into a classroom lecture. I can remember teaching unit on Cultural Mosaic, and we were able to incorporate this lesson around Hispanic Heritage Month. The students were very engaged in lessons about Frida Kahlo and Cesar Chavez. Not only were they able to learn about people, but we were able to learn about sports in the Hispanic Community. The Hispanic students in the class and those within the school were so excited to see artwork displaying their culture. This was a direct reflection of promoting diversity and making others feel a part of the larger image-yet exemplifying academic learning. These are lessons that in years to come will remain at the forefront of a student's learning map. These are difference making techniques that will increase the spectrum of learning and warrant itself to successful gains in the academic setting. The simplest gestures of building on the most amazing relationships to win student success. Is it happening in one day or one setting? No, but it is happening, and the result is sure to be amazing and will have a lasting influence on your scholars.

Show Up for Events and
4 Give Recognition Big & Small

Teachers are remarkably busy people, and they seldom have any time to enjoy life beyond tasks from school that usually follow them home each day. It is important to remember that educators are parents, spouses, siblings, etc. In addition, educators are also working more than one job to ensure they can afford the cost of living. However, with all the obligations, educators are still available to show up for their students. If you live in a small-town community this may be easily accomplished because it is possible you may have a child or other family member or close family friend who shares the same sports team with your student, dance team, or 4-H program. In this way, you can sometimes show up at events.

However, if you are in a larger city, life and traffic may not afford you this opportunity so easily. How can you then show up? It can be done by asking questions about performances. Showing interest goes a long way. It is like being there because the students will understand you were not able to attend, but your heart and mind were in tune to what they had going on outside of class. Just as adults would like support from people in their inner circle, students desire attention and support. If you only support them with in class remediation, tutorial services, or enrichment, they are sure to feel that all that matters to you is how they perform on a data driven sheet, which typically only makes you, as the teacher look good, and the district look good. Why not make everyone look and feel good by a simple gesture of offering your time and attention to students outside the daily lectures and classroom instruction.

Recognition.

Recognition comes in a form of praise and acknowledgement for doing something great. When one accomplishes a specific task, they are recognized. Recognition can be given in various areas when dealing with students. You can recognize a child for scoring a high grade on an assessment, for completing his or her homework, for obtaining mastery on an assessment, for competing in a science or reading fair, for having perfect attendance, or for joining one of the distinguished clubs in the school. What about the child who will never see any of these accolades? How can he or she be recognized?

To recognize a student for even the simplest things are monumental. For example, if a child sweeps the classroom floor or washes the lunchroom table, he or she deserves recognition for a job well done. I was taught to grow up to be that best at whatever I was doing, even if it was taking out the garbage because there is advancement for even the sanitation worker. Some students may not have what it takes to be an honor roll student, and some students may not have anyone at home to wash his or her clothes or have running water to ensure they are able to be present for school and obtain perfect attendance. In this way, we must meet students where they are and let them know you are still deserving of recognition. When this happens, they are again buying in to you and aim to please you in every aspect-even academic where in previous encounters they may have fallen short. The result of this approach is subtle growth. Any growth is good because eventually this will sprout into a beautiful garden with endless opportunities.

5 TEACH

Now that relationships have been structured, and the foundation is strong, you need to just continue to teach your scholars. You may have students who are not at grade level, but know that at this point, they want to invest in you just as much as you have invested in them.

Some educators will encourage you to only teach your low academic learners on the grade level they are able to perform. As a veteran teacher, I would like to encourage you to raise the bar. These students have found someone who cares and someone who believes in them. They are going to work hard for you. They are going to look for ways to gain your attention and recognition.

You have taken a simple note, not written at the start of the year, to gain the likeness of a once-isolated student who, just like you, had been going through the process of insanity. They were repeating the same cycles. Mark is no longer getting into trouble. Mark is no longer labeled as the student who does not have a care for his learning or his future. Mark now believes in himself, and he believes in the one person who took a chance at making him a better student and person. You can now come into your classroom and teach effective lessons without the worry of behavior problems interrupting the day. No longer will you be bogged down daily with stress. You are now able to breathe a sense of fresh air.

TEACH LOVE INSPIRE

Your students will admire you so much that you will witness them wanting to participate more in classroom projects and discussions. They feel they are no longer in a classroom, but they are now in a home—or what we want to view as a safe place. The climate is warm and inviting; the culture is promoting diversity, and the family is well blended. Love is in the atmosphere, and knowledge is brewing softly in the air.

Student mastery is now at its utmost highest peak because you have made learning fun and inviting. The student who needed help all along is no longer ashamed of asking you or his or her peers for assistance. Sue, who was once the model student, sees competition, and she is working harder. All these gestures are bringing successful gains into the academic setting. TEACH the lesson, but do not forget to TEACH the student and not with the student. Every single child deserves someone in their corner who they can go to for years to come for mentorship and guidance, and a little extra tutorial service. Will you be that person? Will you be that champion or scapegoat?

Watch Academic and Student 6 Wellbeing SOAR

A gardener once told me that the best part of the harvest season is sitting back, watching the fruits of his labor go into full rotation. I did not understand the part of rotation, but I knew harvest time was a time for gathering blessings physically and spiritually. He explained that rotation dealt with being able to watch all those you are connected to, and even those you are not connected to, enjoy the blessing of your dedication and hard work.

As an educator, you can watch the labor of your hard work at end-of-year celebrations, graduations, in the community, and through social media posts of big and small accomplishments.

Being told a student went one step further in performance is a win; being told a student successfully overcame the plague that seemed to encompass his or her family is a win; being told a student you once taught became a teacher just like you is a win; being told a student successfully completed a trade program or successfully obtained an institution of higher learning degree is a win; and being told a student who was deemed to spend his or her life in prison due to actions as youth is now a profound community leader or deacon of his church is a win.

There are so many wins associated with building a foundation with students and establishing a home front. Building takes time, but it is worth every building block poured into the scholars you have been called to lead.

When you are asked to speak at a baccalaureate service, an ordination service, a wedding reception, or invited to a baby shower or birthday gathering, or an induction ceremony, remember the recognitions matter, no matter how big or small.

CONCLUSION

Now that you have the tools needed to build effective relationships with your scholars, how do you plan to move forward? Will you move in a rush and continue the process of insanity, or will you slow down and carefully ensure the foundation is layered smoothly and intact? It all starts with you. No youth is too far gone, and no Mark is too far out of touch or too low in his or her academics that you cannot reach them.

I challenge you to make a pledge to pour foundations that will not only build up your classroom, but I challenge you to encourage others on your hall to be a champion and a contractor for building positive relationships in the classroom. Only when this happens will our youth feel they have someone who believes in them. In addition, they will have a passion to be in class every day, taking part in the learning experience. Successful gains will come from every angle, and the educational system will see a decrease in student referrals and student dropout rates. Lectures are good. But what is learning without student engagement and input? You can make learning fun; you can have an influence on the life of your students.

You cannot build these relationships in one day. It takes time. Time means everything. Remember, slow and steady wins the race. Heroes are not just in movies; they are also inside the classroom. Let your heroism show! Do not boast of your heroism, because it will speak for itself in the success stories of your scholars. Answer the call, not the career, and in that you will have made all the difference.

EDUCATION IS KEY

ABOUT
me

Ms. Demetric Blankinship is a native of Bay Springs, MS. She is an eleventh-year educator and published author. Demetric enjoys spending time with her family, exploring the Word of God, reading motivational and self-help books, and writing. As an educator, Demetric has shifted her focus to implementing meaningful ways to secure qualified and resolute educators in classrooms. Her platform is centered around promoting student social, mental, and physical well-being, while yet driving student academic achievement. Demetric's primary focus has become "building impactful relationships-one step at a time."

NOTES

....

....

....

....

....

....

....

....

....

NOTES

....

....

....

....

....

....

....

....

....

....

www.ingramcontent.com/pod-product-compliance
Lightning Source LLC
Chambersburg PA
CBHW052124030426
42335CB00025B/3103